Easy Paper Crafts in 5 Steps

Enslow Elementary
an imprint of
Enslow Publishers, Inc.
40 Industrial Road
Box 398
Berkeley Heights, NJ 07922
USA

http://www.enslow.com

Note to Teachers and Parents: Crafts are prepared using air-drying clay. Please follow package directions. Children may use color clay or they may paint using poster paint once clay is completely dry. The colors used in this book are suggestions. Children may use any color clay, cardboard, pencils, or paint they wish. Let them use their imaginations!

Enslow Elementary, an imprint of Enslow Publishers, Inc.
Enslow Elementary® is a registered trademark of Enslow Publishers, Inc.

Translated from the Spanish edition by Ian Grenzeback, edited by Jaime Ramírez-Castilla, of Strictly Spanish, LLC. Edited and produced by Enslow Publishers, Inc.

Library of Congress Cataloging-in-Publication Data

Llimós Plomer, Anna.
  [Papel. English]
  Easy paper crafts in 5 steps / Anna Llimós.
     p. cm.— (Easy crafts in 5 steps)
  Summary: "Presents easy art crafts made with paper that can be made in 5 steps"—Provided by publisher.
  Includes bibliographical references and index.
  ISBN-13: 978-0-7660-3087-9
  ISBN-10: 0-7660-3087-3
  1. Paper work—Juvenile literature. I. Title.
  TT870.L6213 2007
  745.54—dc22
                                  2007002431

Originally published in Spanish under the title *Papel*.
Copyright © 2005 PARRAMÓN EDICIONES, S.A., - World Rights.
Published by Parramón Ediciones, S.A., Barcelona, Spain.
Text and development of the exercises: Anna Llimós
Photographs: Nos & Soto

Printed in Spain

10 9 8 7 6 5 4 3 2 1

To Our Readers: We have done our best to make sure all Internet Addresses in this book were active and appropriate when we went to press. However, the author and the publishers have no control over and assume no liability for the material available on those Internet sites or on other Web sites they may link to. Any comments or suggestions can be sent by e-mail to comments@enslow.com or to the address on the back cover.

Every effort has been made to locate all copyright holders of material used in this book. If any errors or omissions have occurred, corrections will be made in future editions of this book.

Contents

Dragon

MATERIALS

Poster board
Garland of tissue paper
Clear tape
Black marker
Colored pencils
Dowel or skewer
String
Scissors

1 Draw two parts of the dragon's head on poster board. Cut them out.

2 Draw the teeth with a colored pencil. Draw the face details with a black marker.

3 Cut the tongue out of poster board. Tape it to the bottom of the head.

4 Attach both parts of the dragon's head to one end of the garland using clear tape.

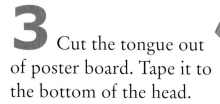

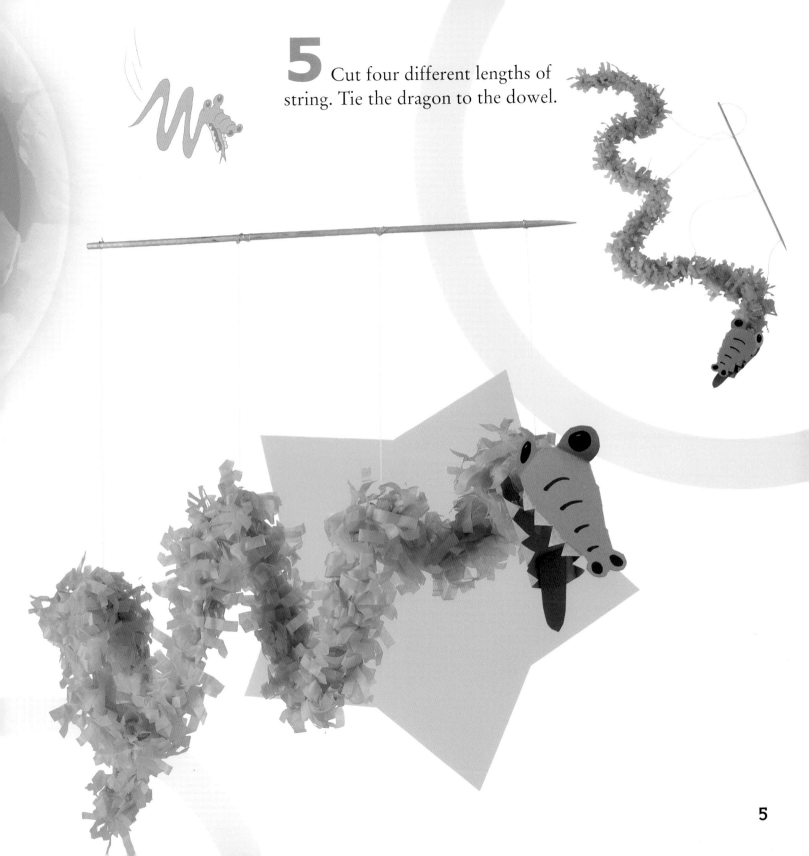

5 Cut four different lengths of string. Tie the dragon to the dowel.

Classroom

MATERIALS

Poster board
Square stickers
Colored pencils
Black fine-tip marker
White glue
Scissors
Ruler

1 Fold one piece
of poster board in half.
On another piece of poster board
make two tabs. Put together the classroom.

2 Stick the square stickers like
floor tiles on another rectangle of
poster board. Place it in the classroom.

3 For the chalkboard, glue a small rectangle of
poster board onto a bigger piece. Draw a simple
picture on it.

4 Cut out two strips of poster board of different sizes. Fold the ends of the larger one, and you will have a table. You can make a chair using the smaller one with just three folds.

5 Make some papers for the desk, and then place everything inside the classroom.

Bowl

Streamers
White glue
Glue wash
Paintbrush

1 Tightly roll up one color of streamer. Glue the end.

2 Glue the end of a another color streamer to it. Roll this one around the first streamer.

3 Repeat step 2 with two more colors of streamer.

8

4 Repeat the previous steps as many times as you wish until you get a large circle.

5 Press down in the center of the circle with your thumbs. Pull up the sides of the bowl as much as you like. If you wish, cover the bowl with a glue wash to make it stronger.

9

Apple

MATERIALS

Poster board
Crepe paper
Colored pencils
Black marker
Clear tape
Hole punch
Scissors
Ruler

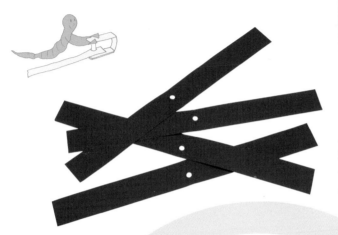

1 Cut four strips of poster board. Make a hole in the middle of each one.

2 Put a little roll of crepe paper through the holes in the strips. Tape it on the bottom.

3 Join the ends of each strip with clear tape. You will have an apple!

4 Draw and cut a leaf out of poster board. Tape the leaf to the apple.

5 Draw, color, and cut a worm out of poster board. Place the worm among the strips.

Bag Puppet

MATERIALS

Brown paper lunch bag
Construction paper
Crepe paper
Round stickers
Black marker
White glue
Scissors

1 Draw the hands and face of the puppet on a piece of paper and cut them out. Draw eyes, a nose, and a mouth on the face.

2 Draw a dress on paper and cut it out. Decorate it with round stickers.

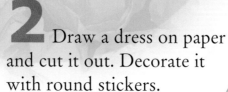

3 For the legs, cut out two strips of paper. Decorate them with stripes. Cut some shoes out of paper and glue them on the legs.

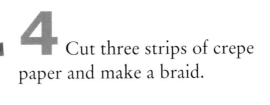

4 Cut three strips of crepe paper and make a braid.

5 Glue all the pieces of the doll on the paper bag, leaving the opening at the bottom.

13

Elephant

MATERIALS

Poster board
Crepe paper
Round stickers
Star-shaped sticker
Colored pencils
White glue
Scissors
Ruler

1 Draw and cut out a
rectangle of poster board with two tabs.
One tab will have fringe that will be the tail, and the
other is where you will glue the elephant's head.

2 Fold the ends of the rectangle.
Draw the legs and color the tail.

3 Glue the folded ends
together. This is the
elephant's body.

14

4 Draw the head and cut it out. Draw the details. Glue some tusks made from poster board on the back. Glue the head on the body.

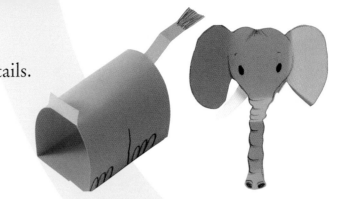

5 For the elephant's blanket, cut out a rectangle of crepe paper and make a fringe. Decorate it with colored stickers.

Basket

1 Place two strips of crepe paper in the shape of an "X." Glue the box on top of them.

2 Cut each of the lengths that stick out from the box into four thinner strips.

3 Cut strips of crepe paper of a different color. Glue the ends to the box. Weave them through the crepe paper on the box.

16

4 Run the extra strips into the box and glue them. Line the interior with more crepe paper. The basket will have a more finished look.

5 Make a handle out of a strip of poster board wrapped with the crepe paper. Glue it to the inside of the basket.

Bus

MATERIALS

Poster board
Construction paper
Cellophane
Black marker
White glue
Scissors
Pencil

1 Draw a bus on the poster board and cut it out. Cut out the windows.

2 Draw and cut out the wheels and lights of the bus. Glue them on. Draw license plate numbers with a black marker.

3 Put the bus on top of a piece of poster board. Mark the windows with a pencil. Draw a person in each one with a black marker.

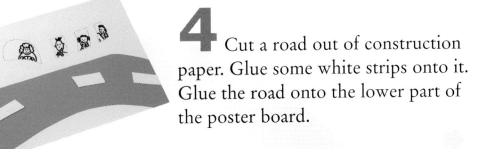

4 Cut a road out of construction paper. Glue some white strips onto it. Glue the road onto the lower part of the poster board.

5 Glue a piece of cellophane onto the back of the bus. Glue the bus onto the poster board so that the windows match the spaces already drawn.

Bird

MATERIALS

Thin paper
White glue
Scissors
Ruler

1 Cut out a square of paper. If you wish, use colored paper.

2 Fold four corners of the square into the center.

3 Turn the paper over and fold the corners into the center.

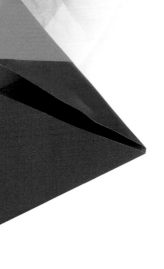

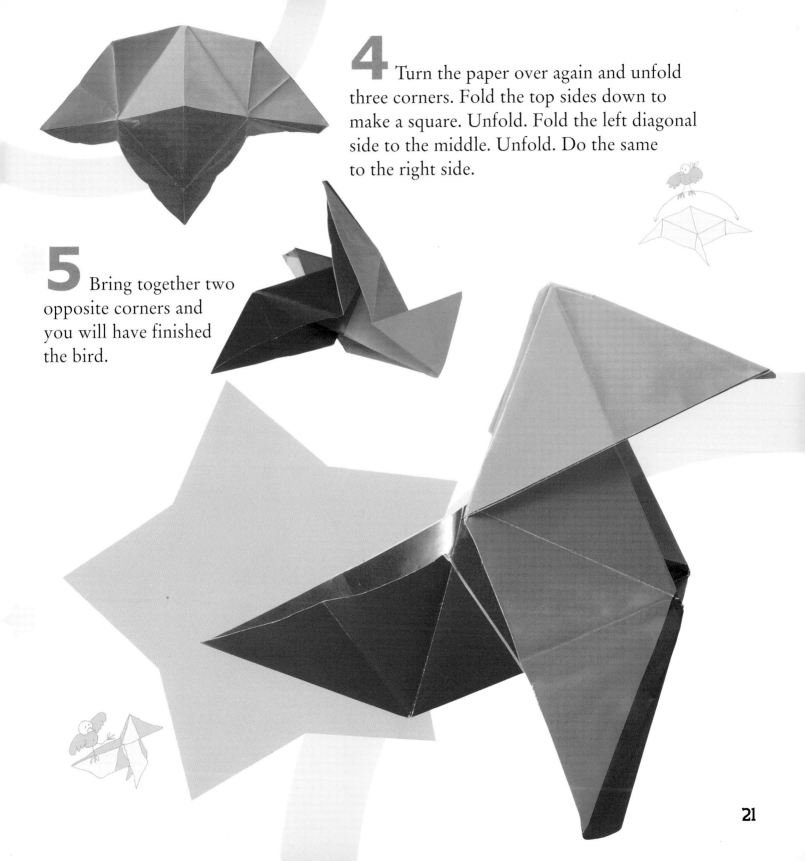

4 Turn the paper over again and unfold three corners. Fold the top sides down to make a square. Unfold. Fold the left diagonal side to the middle. Unfold. Do the same to the right side.

5 Bring together two opposite corners and you will have finished the bird.

Jungle

1 Draw a line near the bottom of the poster board. Cut a long slit.

2 Draw grass on paper and cut it out. Glue it at the bottom of the poster board. Be careful to only put glue below the slot.

3 Draw a trunk on paper, the top of the tree on poster board, and a sun on paper. Cut them out.

4 Cut some figures out of the old magazine. Glue everything on the poster board landscape.

5 Cut animals from the old magazine and glue them onto craft sticks. Put them through the slit in the cardboard and move them.

23

Trumpet

MATERIALS

Poster board
Gift wrap
Tissue paper
Whistle
Black marker
Clear tape
White glue
Scissors
Ruler

1 Draw and cut a cone shape out of poster board.

2 Cover one side of the poster board with gift wrap.

3 Glue the sides together to make a cone. Attach the whistle to the small opening with clear tape.

4 Cut a wide strip of tissue paper and make a fringe.

5 Glue the strip of tissue paper to the wide opening of the cone.

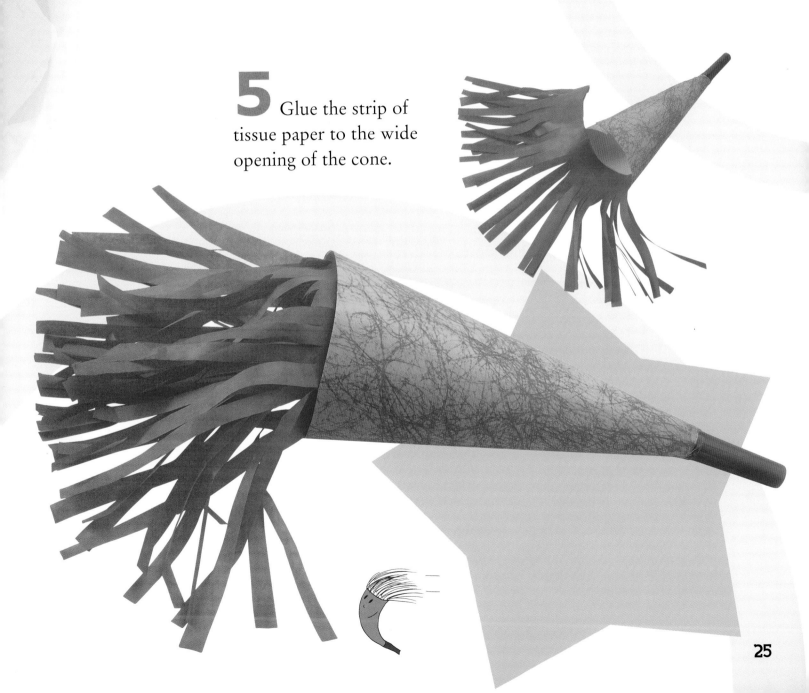

Day and Night

MATERIALS

Poster board
Round stickers
Star-shaped stickers
White glue
Paper fastener
Scissors
Ruler

1 Cut out a small rectangle at the bottom of two pieces of poster board. Cut a rectangular window in the middle of one of them.

2 Draw some mountains and grass on poster board. Cut them out. Glue the two pieces under the window on the red poster board.

3 Now make a few little houses out of poster board. Glue them over the mountains.

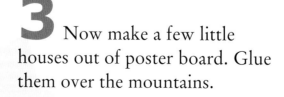

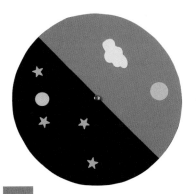

4 Cut a circle and semicircle out of poster board. Glue the semicircle on the circle. Put a moon and some stars on one half, and a sun and a cloud on the other half. Poke a paper fastener through the middle.

5 Use the paper fastener to attach the circle to the solid piece of cardboard. Glue the other cardboard on top, allowing the circle to spin.

Butterfly

MATERIALS

Poster board
Tissue paper
Cellophane
Black marker
White glue
Scissors

1 Draw the outline of a butterfly on poster board and cut it out.

2 Cut out two pieces of tissue paper and two of another color. Glue them to the wings of the butterfly.

3 Finish decorating the wings with torn pieces of tissue paper. Decorate the body with strips of the tissue paper.

4 Cut another butterfly out of cellophane a little bit bigger than the poster board one. Glue the cellophane behind the poster board butterfly.

5 Draw eyes and a mouth on a circle of poster board. Glue on the antennas made of poster board. Glue the head onto the body.

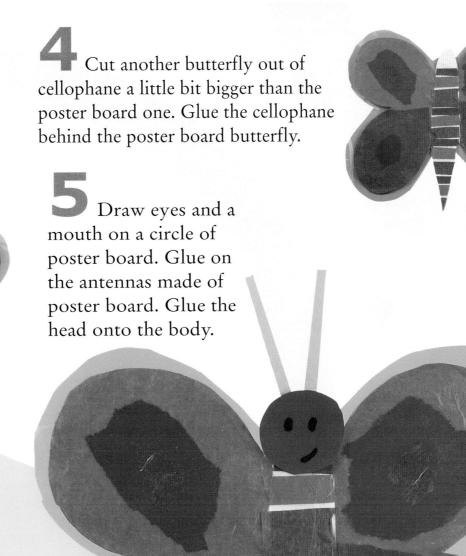

Surprise Card

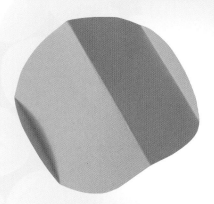

1 Cut a circular shape (the face) out of poster board. Fold it in half and on the sides.

2 Draw the clown's lips and nose on construction paper and cut them out. Make the mouth and eyes out of poster board. Glue everything onto the face. Finish the details with a black marker and a red pencil.

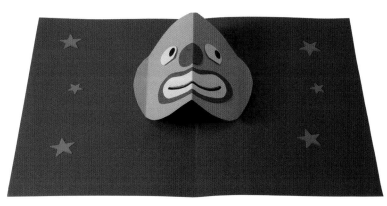

3 Fold a piece of poster board in half. Decorate it with star-shaped stickers. Center the face on the poster board and glue down the sides.

4 Cut two strips of construction paper. Make an accordion out of them.

5 Glue the ends of the accordion below the face. Cut two pieces from the garland of tissue paper. Glue them on for the hair.

Read About

Books

Boursin, Didier. *Paper Folding Fun.* Milwaukee, Wisc.: Gareth Stevens Pub., 2006.

Doney, Meryl. *Paper Crafts.* Milwaukee, Wisc.: Gareth Stevens Pub., 2004.

Rhatigan, Joe, and Rain Newcomb. *Paper Fantastic: 50 Creative Projects to Fold, Cut, Glue, Paint & Weave.* New York: Lark Books, 2004.

Internet Addresses

Crafts for Kids at Enchanted Learning
<http://www.enchantedlearning.com/crafts/>

Kids Craft Weekly
<http://www.kidscraftweekly.com/>

Index

Easy to Hard

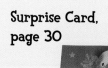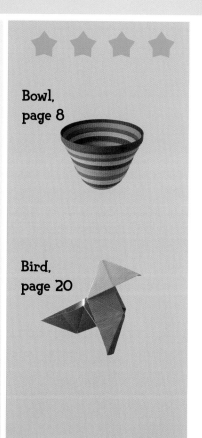